FORGIVENESS REMEMBERS

Paul Farren & Robert Miller

First published in Great Britain in 2017

Instant Apostle
The Barn
1 Watford House Lane
Watford
Herts
WD17 1BJ

British Library Cataloguing-in-Publication Data

A catalogue record for this book is available from the British Library

This book and all other Instant Apostle books are available from Instant Apostle:

Website: www.instantapostle.com

E-mail: info@instantapostle.com

ISBN 978-1-909728-67-7

Printed in Great Britain

Instant Apostle is a pioneering publishing house that exists to inspire followers of Jesus and promote the values of His Kingdom in the world.

Instant Apostle was founded to publish books by writers who are passionate about addressing diverse social issues from a Kingdom perspective – in any and every genre. Whether it is faith-building autobiography, riveting fiction, engaging study in Christian mindfulness or compassionate response to mental health problems, if a book is well written, original and authentic you will find it with us. We want to share Kingdom values with everyone, and publish titles that cross into secular markets, particularly in adults' and children's fiction.

Instant Apostle books engage with varied and poignant subjects, from child sex-trafficking and autism to the plight of asylum seekers and the challenges of young people growing up in the social media age. These are books by informed, creative and sometimes opinionated people that demolish stale paradigms and foster faith in Jesus.

Working with established writers and actively welcoming new authors, Instant Apostle seeks out prophetic voices that will change the way readers young and old understand God's Kingdom and see the world! Are you ready to join us?

Share the passion. Get reading. Get writing. Get published!

instant
apostle

To Liz and Cyril
And
Enda

Contents

Contents

Acknowledgements

It is never easy to write a book, and to write a book with another person makes it even more difficult. When we began this project we were clear that we wanted the book to be written in one voice. It would have failed in its aim if it were two separate voices in one book.

We are deeply indebted to Mary Murphy for her role in making our aim a reality. Mary's long and patient work ensured that this book reveals the truth that we share the same vision of forgiveness. Our greatest thanks is reserved for Mary.

We are also deeply indebted both to His Eminence Cormac Cardinal Murphy O'Connor, the retired Archbishop of Westminster, and to the Rt Rev and Rt Honourable Dr Richard Chartres, the retired Bishop of London, for their generosity in writing the forewords.

Furthermore, we would like to thank those who attended the course on forgiveness and who shared so openly.

Indeed we want to thank all those who helped in any way to make this book a reality, and Instant Apostle for publishing it.

Foreword

by The Rt Rev & Rt Hon Dr Richard
Chartres, retired Bishop of London

We cannot change the past, but we are
responsible for how we remember the past. You
do not create a kinder world by enforcing
amnesia and banning any public remembrance
of man's inhumanity to man. But what we
choose to remember shapes the future. In truth,
we remember the future.

That is why this book by Paul Farren and
Robert Miller addresses such a crucial subject
for our generation as the media confronts us
daily with a world full of conflict and hatred.
The authors show us there is another story to
tell, and another way.

In the modern world religious passions have
often played a part in conflict. Contemplating
the rubble of one of our City of London
churches, St Ethelburga, destroyed by a bomb

13

planted by the IRA as part of the sectarian conflict in Ireland, I conceived of a Centre for Preventing and Transforming conflict, especially those with a religious dimension. In the 1990s when I enlisted the Cardinal and Free Church leaders in the project to rebuild the church, which was intended to be a gift to all people of faith, there were many who could not see the point of such a Centre for Reconciliation and Peace. The events of the twenty-first century have changed perceptions and given us painful experience of the reality of and the need for the process of right remembering that moves us towards forgiveness and reconciliation.

It is a hard and difficult task, and reconciliation is not the restoration of some 'untroubled' condition before a conflict; it is the creation of something that would never have been without that conflict. The authors help us to reflect on the process both in our own personal struggles with our need to forgive and be forgiven, and in our communities and national and international life.

Jesus Christ, whom Christians believe is the human face of God, is never a hero for our sectarian causes. His way of self-giving love is the way into 'a wider us', inclusive of all creatures under the heaven, a deeper sense of the deep universal drama beneath and beyond the white noise of every day, and so the way into a better life together.

Foreword

by Cardinal Cormac Murphy O'Connor,
Archbishop Emeritus of Westminster

On 5 October 2016 Pope Francis and Archbishop
Justin Welby issued the Common Declaration. It
was a declaration of hope. It was a challenge to
all Anglicans and Catholics to respect one
another as sisters and brothers who share a
common baptism. While the declaration
acknowledges with sadness the differences that
exist between us, the Archbishop and the Pope
focus on what unites us.

They tell us:

> Wider and deeper than our differences are
> the faith that we share and our common joy
> in the Gospel ... Christians who have come
> to this faith, have encountered Jesus and the
> victory of his love in their own lives, and are
> impelled to share the joy of this Good News
> with others ... The world must see us

witnessing to this common faith in Jesus by acting together.[1]

In this little book Robert and Paul have come together to reflect upon the call to forgiveness, which is a universal call. Forgiveness is not easy. In the world today that is divided and fractured in so many ways, we need to courageously explore forgiveness as a key element on the road to peace. Peace is not achieved by proving that we are stronger than our enemy. Peace is achieved when we respect our enemy and forgive them. This is much easier said than done.

This book, drawn from the personal experience of the authors and their communities, is full of practical thinking for anybody and everybody who struggles to forgive, and I warmly commend it.

---

[1] 'Full text: Common Declaration of Pope Francis and the Archbishop of Canterbury', *Catholic Herald*, http://www.catholicherald.co.uk/news/2016/10/05/full-text-common-declaration-of-pope-francis-and-the-archbishop-of-canterbury/ (accessed 15th February 2017).

Introduction

The Church of Ireland Church, Christ Church, is situated at the bottom of Brooke Park in Derry/Londonderry. Across the road from it is St Eugene's Catholic Cathedral. Traditionally, each church has gone about its Christian business without any reference to the other. How strange it is that two Christian churches sited so closely together should operate so independently of each other. Yes, doctrinal differences do exist between our Christian churches, but oughtn't our focus to be on what unites us rather than on what divides us? Jesus, to whom we are all committed as Christians, crossed the road regularly to reach out compassionately to those in need, regardless of difference. He reached out His healing hands to the marginalised, the ostracised, the diseased, the outcast, the sinner. Jesus crossed the road fearlessly and embraced all.

We came to our two parishes at about the same time, Robert to Christ Church and Paul to St Eugene's. We began to meet with each other on a regular basis, and became friends. Our friendship over the years has in no way threatened our individual identities, but it has challenged us to acknowledge the times when we retreat to the comfort of our group, thankful, perhaps, for the existence of the road which runs between us.

As our friendship grew, we had many discussions about the divided society in which we both live, a society divided politically and religiously, with politics and religion often appearing as uncomfortably close bedfellows. We questioned whether it was possible for lasting peace to be achieved in such a divided society. Could a sharing of political power alone be enough? Surely real peace demanded an honest, creative working together at a religious level as well?

Looking at the causes of division and conflict within our society, we came to the painful conclusion that hatred can all too readily be dressed up to appear acceptable, and that forgiveness is the most difficult reality to accept on the road to peace. At that point in our deliberations, this little book began to take shape.

Crossing the road to meet with each other in friendship has sometimes been challenging; more often than not it's been rewarding. It's been a source of great joy in the sharing of our commitment to proclaiming the gospel of Jesus; it's been a source of pain in our reluctant acceptance of the divisions between our churches.

An example of both the joy and the pain was borne home to us very powerfully at the end of January 2014. Robert won the Christmas Draw in St Eugene's Cathedral Parish. With some of the money he won he planned a trip to Rome and he invited me to accompany him. We will leave the reader to appreciate the irony. We both certainly did! It was three days of fun and faith and prayer. On one of the days we visited a shop which sold vestments with a view to making some purchases, and at that moment hard reality hit home. Despite our friendship, despite all that united us, back home Robert would wear his vestments in his church with his people, and across the road, Paul would wear his vestments in his church with his people.

We have looked at the road between our churches and reflected on how it symbolises the reality of division. But we had encountered one another in friendship; we had discovered that friendship with the one who is different is not only possible, it is also life-giving. Was there a road to be found, we wondered, that led from hate to peace? In time we discovered a road which, we believe, has the potential to lead us out of the darkness of hate into the light of peace. This book explores that road. It is a hard road and it requires much courage to negotiate its twists and turns, because it is never going to be a straight road; at best it is going to be a spiral: spiralling up to the light of peace from the darkness of hatred. It is a road that needs to visit places like pity, compassion, forgiveness and grace.

We believe it is a road worth travelling if we are to become the people God intended us to be: people living out His precept of love; people unthreatened by difference; generous in spirit; haters only of the walls which have divided us for far too long and which, if we are open to the flow of God's grace, we can, and will, demolish together.

For further reflection

- How do friendship and faith interact in your life?

- What does a call to honest and creative working together at a religious level look like in your situation?

- Do you think forgiveness is a difficult reality on the road to peace?

Chapter 1
Hate

The ultimate weakness of violence is that it is a
descending spiral.
Dr Martin Luther King Jr

'I hate them and hell won't be full until they are
all in it.'

'I can't even bear to look at her.'

'I despise the weasel.'

'I wouldn't even spit on him.'

These are all expressions of hatred spoken in
terrible anger. From time to time as ministers of
religion we have heard these expressions and
others like them. We have heard them from
members of our community about others. We
have heard them from people when they are
speaking about another family member. In some
ways the people who speak these words can be

at an advantage, because even though they are coming from a place of terrible anger, even though they are consumed by hatred, they at least are able to articulate their hatred, and that can be the first step in doing something about it. Many of us suppress our feelings of hatred or deny their existence. It is not right, not good, we think, to feel hatred, and so we bury these 'bad' feelings under a weight of guilt. Yet hate is a very real emotion that exists at some level in most of us. Paradoxically, when it is denied it can grow in strength and power. It can dictate our actions which can become destructive, violent.

'He pushed me first!' is an aggressive phrase familiar to parents, teachers and youth leaders across the globe.

'She pushed me and so I pushed her back!'

There seems to be a certain logic in retaliation; it evens things out. But we live in a world that takes the 'principle' of retaliation to a much more dangerous level and instead of a push, retaliation takes the murderous form of bombs and bullets. Our community here in Northern Ireland, which was and continues to be predominantly Christian, fought with itself.

We pushed people apart, divided them into 'them' and 'us'. We were violent. We were destructive. There was hatred. There was mistrust. That hatred hasn't gone away. It manifests itself in the ugly way we treat people who have come to live among us from other countries: with repulsion and rejection and often with violence.

It may seem strange to introduce a book about peace with a discussion about hatred, but any serious journey needs to be clear about both its starting point and its destination. When we look at our community, and indeed the world around us, we see many broken relationships. Hatred breaks relationships. Hate is very powerful. In its implacable determination to survive at all costs, it spreads its tentacles of fear, mistrust and suspicion. It urges us towards the conviction that there is nothing to be done, that the 'other' will never change; and it is always, hate insists, the 'other' who needs to change. When we hate, we push people away, one way or another. When we actively push another person away, we repulse that person, openly expressing our hate-filled and, perhaps, violent, intentions towards them. Pushing a person away passively is a more covert rejection of that person: we employ a passive obliteration of the other, a denial of the other's very existence. A priest visiting a prisoner was subjected to insulting words from a warder. On hearing about the incident, the prisoner's response was, 'Don't even ignore him, Father!' In truth, it was hatred that caused the warder to insult the priest, and it was hatred that caused the prisoner's suggestion to deny the very existence of the warder.

Hatred is damaging and destructive; it is life- and soul-denying. A person who had been homeless for a time said he felt wiped out, obliterated, by the many people who walked past him without looking at him, without seeming to notice him. The worst thing he experienced, he said, was not the loss of material possessions, or even the lack of food; it was when he realised he had become a non-person. Society had simply stopped noticing his existence. To have our identity, our personhood, taken from us like that is a cruelly destructive blow. It may be a subtle expression of hatred, but it is nonetheless devastating in its effect.

In Northern Ireland, and in many other places where there has been armed conflict, people become very proficient at identifying the 'other': the one they can hate with impunity. The 'other' can be anyone who is different. The 'other' is my enemy. We claim it is important to know exactly who the 'other' is so that we can avoid giving offence, but the reality at the back of our minds often is that we need to know who the 'other' is in order to stay safe. We are a society emerging from a prolonged period of violence, and that means that we need to pause in order to appreciate where we are exactly on the road to real peace before we can move forward. The rules we fashioned to keep us safe may, at this juncture, be the rules which inhibit forgiveness and lasting peace. Martin Luther King reminds us of the danger of violence in our midst:

> The ultimate weakness of violence is that it is a descending spiral, begetting the very thing it seeks to destroy. Instead of diminishing evil, it multiplies it. Through violence you may murder the liar, but you cannot murder the lie, nor establish the truth. Through violence you murder the

hater, but you do not murder hate. In fact, violence merely increases hate. Returning violence for violence multiplies violence, adding deeper darkness to a night already devoid of stars. Darkness cannot drive out darkness; only light can do that. Hate cannot drive out hate. Only love can do that.[2]

We live in a world at war. In an article in *The Guardian* newspaper in 2002, Eric Hobsbawm said that since 1914, the world had not been at peace, and still was not at peace.[3] The world is at war. There is no doubt about this. The question we must ask is, 'Why?' Why is the world at war? And what, we may ask, has any war in which we are not directly involved, to do with us? A fair question, but we need to step back from particular wars and ask ourselves some other pertinent questions. Why do human beings resort to violence to accomplish their ends? Why do we fight with one another? Why do we hurt one another? Are we attracted to

---

[2] The Rev Dr Martin Luther King Jr, *Where Do We Go From Here? Chaos or Community* ©1967, p. 62 (reading from Beacon Press [Boston, MA] paperback edition).
[3] Eric Hobsbawm, *The Guardian*, 21st February 2002.

hatred? Does hatred and the violence it so often begets hold a dark attraction for humans?

'My community' is a phrase we hear endlessly in Northern Ireland. It is used both inclusively and exclusively. It defines both 'them' and 'us'. As long as we entertain a 'them' and 'us' mentality, we encourage an acceptance of hatred as a way of life. Just imagine the inhabitants of Northern Ireland describing themselves as one community capable of accepting, even celebrating, differences. Would this not mean that we would no longer define ourselves in terms of hatred? We have lived too long holding each other at arm's length, making it impossible to embrace one another. To build a new society we need to see all of our neighbours as 'our' community. We are not seeking a 'one size fits all cultures' solution, but one in which we can recognise that difference should not automatically divide us. Rabbi Jonathan Sacks has written:

War speaks to our most fundamental sense of identity: there is an 'us' and 'them' and no possibility of confusing the two. When, though, enemies shake hands, who is now the 'us' and who is the 'them'? Peace involves a profound crisis of identity. The boundaries of self and other, friend and foe, must be redrawn.[4]

Children are good at doing this. They can redraw boundaries easily because they are not trapped by the power of hatred. They break down barriers naturally. You can see this in public transport in major cities. Cities are impersonal places: people don't, as a rule, speak to one another; they rarely make eye contact. Modern technology allows commuters to insert earphones and listen to music in total isolation and total self-absorption. But we have seen people being seduced away from this self-imposed isolation in a New York subway by a young couple carrying a little baby. We watched the effect the baby had on other people on the subway and it was amazing. One young man proceeded to make faces at the baby to make him smile; another person sitting next to the couple admired the baby and then engaged the mother in conversation. The baby brought strangers together and facilitated a non-

[4] Jonathan Sacks, *The Dignity of Difference* (London: Continuum, 2002) p. 8.

threatening communication. It was easy to marvel at the miracle of his existence, to recognise him as a brother. The strangers had a united focus: the baby. Unity does not need uniformity; we are not all the same. Our sense of identity should come from our belief that every human being is created in the image and likeness of God, and is unique. God gives us life and it is God's desire to be in friendship with every child He creates. The true source of our identity lies in the fact that every human has the same divine parent.

The parable of the Good Samaritan is one of Jesus' more familiar parables.[5] The reason is that it asks a question many of us ask ourselves from time to time: 'Who is my neighbour?' Maybe it would be helpful if we turn Jesus' question to the lawyer on its head and ask instead, 'Who isn't my neighbour?' It might offer us a new perspective. The parable tells us that people saw the injured man, but passed him by. Perhaps we don't need to look at the reasons for their behaviour at this point but simply acknowledge the fact that they saw the man and rejected him.

---

[5] Luke 10:25–37.

He had been violently repulsed by those who had beaten and robbed him and left him for dead. And now his beaten and bloodied body caused others to turn away from him; they, too, left him for dead. The Samaritan, Jesus directs us, is the true neighbour, because when he saw the man lying on the ground, his heart was moved to pity which, in turn, caused him to tenderly bind the poor man's wounds and ensure further care for him. By his actions the Samaritan showed that he was the man's neighbour. The parable presents us with pictures of both repulsion and rejection and how they can collude in an unholy alliance. Our actions and reactions when they are fuelled by hatred can only be destructive.

A number of years ago an Irish department store opened a branch in a town in Northern Ireland. A woman did her shopping there and when she brought it into the house her husband, when he saw the bags, flew into a rage. He took the bagfuls of shopping outside and threw them into the bin. He wasn't going to allow anything Irish into his home. Anything Irish, to his hate-fuelled mind, had to be violently rejected.

When the Rwandan Bishop Nathan Amooti visited Derry/Londonderry a few years ago he spoke about how he was once asked what he'd had to give up in order to be able to forgive. His answer to the question was both simple and compelling. He said he'd had to give up his hate. Too often we share the opinion of the American poet Robert Frost's neighbour, in his poem, 'Mending Wall': interface areas often leave those who live there expressing the view that the better the wall, the better the neighbour. We need, we feel, clear boundaries so we can be certain of who is 'us' and who is 'them'. Those clear boundaries have become our own expression of 'good walls'. If we can see certain people as 'other', then we allow ourselves to build a wall of reasons as to why we should treat them differently. We may see someone as a fellow competitor and that can appear to be pretty harmless, natural, even. However, as we shall see, it can be a very short step from seeing another as a fellow competitor to seeing that person as a threat, and from there to seeing them as an enemy. It is our natural instinct to want to fight our enemy. It is a plausible journey in many ways to go from seeing someone as a brother or a sister to seeing them as a competitor, then as a threat and, finally, as an enemy. This journey has nothing to do with God. It has nothing to do with Jesus. It is a journey Jesus wants us to reject. Jesus does not want us to move beyond seeing each other as brothers and sisters. This is one of the profound challenges we have to face on any journey that seeks to reach forgiveness.

The British philosopher, John Stuart Mill, delivered an inaugural address at the University of St Andrews during which he said, 'Let not anyone pacify his conscience by the delusion that he can do no harm if he takes no part, and forms no opinion. Bad men need nothing more to compass their ends, than that good men should look on and do nothing.'[6] If forgiveness is essential for us to grow and become a community at peace, then hatred, whether it be expressed either as repulsion or rejection, must be addressed. If we remain standing at the signpost to our destination we will never reach it: we need to start walking. St Benedict encouraged his monks to open themselves to

---

[6]Source www.quoteinvestigator.com/2010/12/04/good-men-do/ (accessed 8th December 2016).

God: 'But as we progress in this way of life and in faith, we shall run on the path of God's commandments, our hearts overflowing with the inexpressible delight of love.'[7]

The dream of God, the Good News of Jesus, is that we live in this world as brothers and sisters, children of God. This is what Jesus wants. However, it is a constant struggle to live in that relationship of equality, mutual love and acceptance. An example of how ingrained it is to live with an 'us' and 'them' mentality was revealed at a talk about Northern Ireland 20 years after the IRA ceasefire. One speaker described our society as being like a seesaw. In the past, the Protestant section of our community, he said, felt that it was the dominant force on the seesaw, but now the balance was tipping and seemed to be going in favour of the Catholic section of our community. The speaker felt that in the interests of a healthy community, a balance should be kept between both sides, and then both sides would be happy. But surely this goal would only lead to keeping the 'us' and 'them' alive at either end of a

---

[7] *Rule of St Benedict in English* (Collegeville, MN: The Liturgical Press, 1982) Prologue 49, p. 19.

seesaw, each watching the other to make sure that no advantage was being taken which might ensure dominance? This can't be what living as brothers and sisters means. The seesaw model of community surely only serves to stoke mutual suspicion and a negative watchfulness: 'us' and 'them' in a tense permanent state of competition.

St Paul speaks very directly about competition. In his letter to the Philippians he says, 'There must be no competition among you.'[8]

Paul's vision is for us to be united in love with a common purpose and a common mind. The common purpose he speaks about is lived out as the body of Christ. The common mind he speaks about is the mind of Jesus. He goes on to say, 'Always consider the other person to be better than yourself, so that no person thinks of his own interests first but everybody thinks of other people's interests instead. In your minds you must be the same as Christ Jesus.'[9]

---

[8] Philippians 2:3, The Inclusive Bible (Lanham, MD: Rowman & Littlefield Publishers, 2007).

[9] Philippians 2:1–5, paraphrased.

'There must be no competition among you.' And yet competition appears to exercise a stranglehold on how we live our daily lives. We use it, we say, to increase self-esteem, but isn't our self-esteem only increased if we win?

Competition can become the way that we relate most often to each other.

A child tells her parents: 'I got a B in my test.'

'Good!' respond the parents, but secretly they wonder how many children got an A.

Is a B really good enough?

The person who beats me becomes a threat to me, and doesn't the world try to make us feel more and more as a threat to one another? Do you remember the swine flu outbreak? Not for a moment do we wish to trivialise or undermine the real need there is to prevent the spread of disease; however, our reaction to the swine flu outbreak made each of us view every other person as a deadly threat.

There is a true story that is told about this time. At the beginning of a meeting which included people with learning disabilities, an announcement was made that due to the swine flu, those attending the meeting that morning should refrain from hugging each other or shaking hands. Just after midday, a boy with Down's syndrome proceeded to go around the room hugging people. When he was reminded of the earlier announcement and asked to stop hugging people immediately, he asked, 'Why? Sure isn't the morning over now!'

If we insist on seeing people as threats, we are unable to trust them. We become suspicious of them and their intentions and they can fast take on the coloration of our enemies. We can conceivably take what appears as a logical step from seeing the cute baby in the subway as our brother to seeing him 20 years later, with a beard and different clothing, as our enemy, and the ensuing hatred can drive our actions and our reactions towards him.

At the end of this chapter the question we need to ask ourselves is, 'How can I move from seeing this young man as my enemy to seeing him again as my brother? How do I move from hate-fuelled rejection and repulsion to forgiveness?'

Can we examine our hearts for signs of hatred and repulsion?

Can we see clearly where we are now in order to discern the way ahead?

For further reflection

- Do you think there are situations where you are suppressing feelings of hatred, or where you are denying them?

- How does hate break relationships?

- How would you answer Eric Hobsbawm's question: Does hatred and the violence it so often begets hold a dark attraction for humans?

Chapter 2
Pity

Pity is to soften our hearts towards others.

On *The Late Late Show* on Friday 10th October 2014, Kathleen Chada spoke about how her husband had murdered their two sons and then had tried unsuccessfully to kill himself. She shared how she had looked him in the eye as the court declared him guilty of murder. She said that she could not forgive him for the terrible thing he had done; she would leave that to God. While acknowledging her own inability to forgive her husband, she doesn't block his forgiveness from God. It was an amazing response from a woman going through unimaginable pain. How do we live with the reality that someone has hurt us callously and deliberately? How do we engage with someone who openly threatens us? How do we deal with someone we see as our enemy, someone we hate?

A common answer to that question is that we should seek justice, take revenge, give as good as we get. Revenge seems a natural reaction to someone who has inflicted pain on us: we want to make that person pay for what they have done. The desire for revenge is ingrained in us, often at an unconscious level, and we often express it in terms of justice.

We see and hear the same message of revenge in our society and from its leaders all the time. The day after Osama bin Laden was captured and murdered, an obscenely smug headline in one of the papers read, 'We got the b*****d!' And when Saddam Hussein was murdered, a headline screamed, 'Rot in Hell.'

The US vice president, Joe Biden, warned the Islamic State militant extremists that they should know that the US would follow them to hell's gates till they were brought to justice, because hell was where they would be going.[10] An understandable reaction, you may well think, to the atrocity for which the group had just taken responsibility: the beheading of Steven Sotloff and James Foley, a gruesome and horrific act, and surely an act for which the perpetrators ought to pay. But the question we must ask is whether it is ultimately helpful to wish them to hell? What does wishing them to hell achieve?

The rhetoric of the world may well be one of revenge: hound the culprits and make them pay; make them suffer as their victims are suffering.

But Kathleen Chada showed in her response that she harboured no desire for revenge.

It is difficult to rid our hearts of all traces of hatred; difficult to take even the first step. It can seem as if we are offering the guilty person an unconditional release from the prison in which we know in our hearts they belong. We are being submissive, we worry, and letting the real victim down. Society can see forgiveness as a trivialising of the evil done. Is this true? Is

---

[10] *Daily Mail*, 3rd September 2014, by Sophie Jane Evans for *MailOnline* and David Martosko, US political editor for *MailOnline*.

forgiveness the action of the weak? If this is so, then what is the right response to the one who has hurt us? What ought our response be to the one who has offered us violence? What do we do with our need to wreak vengeance on the one who has shown himself to be our enemy? What do we do with our anger?

In an enclosed community like a monastery or a convent, tensions between individuals can become magnified. St Thérèse of Lisieux, in her autobiography, reflects on her struggles with another nun:

Formerly one of our nuns managed to irritate me whatever she did or said. … As I did not want to give way to my natural dislike for her, I told myself that charity should not only be a matter of feeling but should show itself in deeds. So I set myself to do for this sister what I should have done for someone I loved most dearly. Every time I met her, I prayed for her and offered God all her virtues and her merits. … I did not remain content with praying a lot for this nun who caused me so much disturbance. I tried to do as many things for her as I could, and whenever I was tempted to speak unpleasantly to her, I made myself give her a pleasant smile and tried to change the subject. ...

When I was violently tempted by the devil and if I could slip away without her seeing my inner struggle, I would flee like a soldier deserting the battlefield. And after all this she asked me one day with a beaming face: 'Sister Thérèse, will you please tell me what attracts you so much to me? You give me such a charming smile whenever we meet.' Ah! It was Jesus hidden in the depths of her soul who attracted me, Jesus who makes the bitterest things sweet![11]

St Thérèse embraced and engaged with rather than excluded and rejected. She made herself accept that the light of Christ shone in the depths of this disagreeable person as brightly as within any other. This is the first step in beginning to encounter the reality and humanity of the other person.

When we hate others we sometimes call them animals: we dehumanise them. We keep them at

---

[11] St Thérèse of Lisieux, *The Story of a Soul* (Washington DC: ICS Publications, 1996), pp. 126–127.

arm's length. When we begin the shift from hating them, we are, in effect, seeing them as human beings, but seeing them as human beings can pose difficult challenges for us. Yet if we do not address the reality of what to do about someone who has harmed us, we allow our hatred to grow, to become all-consuming, and we ourselves may be the first casualty of that hatred. It is in this light that we see how important forgiveness is.

To sustain harbouring an enemy requires energy, time and focus. It prohibits us from living life to the full; it holds us hostage. What can we do? It takes a huge leap to go from hating an enemy to forgiving that enemy, and for many it is too big a leap. Perhaps we should think in terms of steps instead of leaps. Maybe the first step is towards pity, but is this a manageable step?

Pity is a feeling we may not like very much. We rarely like to be at the receiving end of pity. There something condescending about it, we think. Accepting pity can be difficult, and yet, to reach out to another in pity can be a powerful act, even a courageous act. In the Roman Catholic tradition, Veronica emerges as a significant person for Jesus on the road to Calvary. She takes pity on His suffering and she rushes forward to wipe His bleeding face with her veil. This was a remarkably courageous thing to do in the face of a hostile, jeering crowd. Veronica, moved to pity, put the suffering of another before her own safety.

Polish priest Maximilian Kolbe died in Auschwitz as prisoner 16770 on 14th August 1941. When a prisoner escaped from the camp, the Nazis would select ten others to die from enforced starvation in a vengeful act of reprisal for the escape. On this occasion, one of the ten selected, Franciszek Gajowniczek, cried: 'My wife! My children! I will never see them again!' Then Maximilian Kolbe stepped forward and asked to die in the distraught man's place. Knowing he faced certain death, Maximilian Kolbe nevertheless reached out in pity to his fellow prisoner, a pity so powerful that it resulted in an act of amazing altruism and courage.[12]

In both of these examples, pity came from a place of love. But is it possible to pity an enemy

---

[12] http://auschwitz.dk/Kolbe.htm (accessed 8th December 2016).

when our hearts are unmoved by love? What can motivate us to show pity to an unloved one who has done us wrong? How do we move from hate to pity? It is a hugely difficult step to take. Is it possible to pity the rapist, the thief? Is it possible to pity Islamic State? They cause others to suffer, so shouldn't they suffer too? Many of us struggle with the reality of suffering. For example, we struggle to understand why a person who has always lived a good life should be visited by tragedy. 'How can this good person be afflicted with such pain?' we often hear. They don't deserve it. The good should be protected from suffering, we think. The concept of justice would seem to suggest that the bad should suffer while the good should not.

A commentator on the Psalms once said that Psalm 1 is the psalmist's vision of how things ought to be, and the other 149 are his response to the world he sees as he looks around him.

After the tower collapses in Siloam and a group of Galileans are murdered by Pilate, Jesus is asked if this has happened because these people were worse sinners than others. Jesus' reply is 'No!'

Now there were some present at that time who told Jesus about the Galileans whose blood Pilate had mixed with their sacrifices. Jesus answered, 'Do you think that these Galileans were worse sinners than all the other Galileans because they suffered this way? I tell you, no! But unless you repent, you too will perish. Or those eighteen who died when the tower ... fell on them – do you think they were more guilty than all the others living in Jerusalem? I tell you, no! But unless you repent, you too will perish.[13]

Suffering is not the punishment meted out by God to evildoers. We may never fully understand why suffering seems to invade some people's lives more than others, but what we do know is that God is at the heart of all suffering. His tenderness and love reach out to us when our long night is at its darkest. He offers us, through suffering, the gift of the open door leading to profound soulwork, as Richard Rohr reminds us: 'Suffering leads you in either of two directions. It can make you very bitter and close you down. Or it can make

---

[13] Luke 13:1–5.

you wise, compassionate, and utterly open – either because your heart has been "softened," or because suffering helps you realize you have nothing more to lose.'[14] John McAreavey, a young man who suffered the terrible, terrible loss of his beautiful bride, murdered while they were honeymooning in Mauritius, has spoken publicly about having miraculously experienced, when he was at his lowest, most despairing ebb, the warmth of God's arms holding him close.

Hatred stifles spiritual and emotional growth. It chokes lives. It hardens hearts, and it deafens ears. But, surely, to live a hate-filled stunted life cut off from the wellsprings of grace is a form of self-inflicted suffering? Only pity can soften our hearts towards those who suffer from hatred.

However, it must be acknowledged that the first step in leaving hatred behind and travelling towards pity is not a step we can take naturally. It is a step that requires a deliberate decision. In many ways it is not logical to move away from

---

[14] Richard Rohr, OFM, *The Naked Now: Learning to See as the Mystics See* (NY: The Crossroad Publishing Co., 2013) p. 125.

hatred. It is not logical to let go of the desire for revenge and, because of its illogicality, it requires God's grace to help us effect that step. It requires God's grace to help us move from the belief that the one who has hurt us is our enemy to the belief that the one who has hurt us is still our brother or our sister. In order to expel the enemy from our lives forever, we may resort to describing them as an animal, but the truth is that person is not an animal. They may have done a terrible thing, but we cannot take away their humanity. God doesn't.

There is a story told about Pope John XXIII when he was Cardinal and Patriarch of Venice. One evening he was having dinner with a number of priests. The priests were discussing a brother priest who had caused a great scandal. They advised the cardinal that he should get rid of the errant priest because of what he had done. The cardinal said nothing for a while. Then he lifted a crystal glass from the table and asked the assembled priests to name the owner of the glass. 'But that is you, cardinal,' the priests responded. 'The glass belongs to you.' The cardinal dropped the glass on the floor and it smashed into pieces. 'Who owns the glass now?'

he asked the priests. They replied, 'It is still your glass, cardinal.'

'It is the same with the priest,' the cardinal said.

The cardinal, with a beautiful clarity, had illustrated the Christian truth that no matter what terrible thing another human being has done, that person is still our brother or our sister. Acknowledging this truth is a step towards pity.

If our brother has done something wrong, something that has harmed us, when we pity him we recognise his humanity. Feeling pity for the one who has harmed us is to acknowledge that, while that person may have treated us inhumanly, in effect, it is their own humanity they have attacked.

Our pity can enable us to ask, 'Why?' Why did they do what they did? What drove them to violence? What drove them to smash relationships? When we ask ourselves questions like this we are moving from seeing the other person as the enemy to seeing them as wounded and in need of healing. Perhaps it is their woundedness and their inability to deal with that woundedness that leads them to lash out at others. There are many wounded people in our world today, and in their distorted cry for attention, for healing, they cause havoc in the lives of others and, perversely, the harm that they cause deepens their own wounds. Hurt people hurt people.

How do we respond to these people's woundedness? We can exploit it and try our best to make it worse, but in so doing, we wound ourselves. Or we can feel pity for their woundedness, sad at their inability or their unwillingness to accept the beauty of their humanity.

Our pity for another person can lead us either to despise them or it can enable us to feel compassion for them. If our pity leads us to despise them, we can grow to hate them for what we perceive as their weakness, and this hatred is only a step away from violence. A vicious circle is already shaping itself.

If our pity leads us into compassion, something very powerful can happen. The journey from pity to compassion can be painful, but it will always lead us into the light of God.

For further reflection

- How do people usually behave when others hurt them?

- What does it look like to pity someone?

- What was the source of Maximilian Kolbe's pity?

- Do you agree that the journey from pity to compassion can be painful but will bear fruit? Why?

Chapter 3
Compassion

What does God's power look like?

In our journey towards forgiveness we must now turn and consider if we have come to an impasse where the whole process falters! It is understandable to hate. It might be possible to have pity. With both hate and pity there still can be a profound separation between the one who has been hurt and the one who has caused the hurt, between perpetrator and victim. The next step, compassion, has the power to heal that separation, but is that a step which is possible for us to take? Is it possible to feel compassion for someone who has harmed us?

In order to answer these vital questions, we need to find an example of someone who showed compassion to those who had inflicted great pain on him or her, and for us the obvious person surely ought to be Jesus. Strangely, as Christians we can often overlook the person of Jesus when we are looking for examples of compassion or forgiveness in the world today. Perhaps we automatically look for more recent examples, or perhaps we perceive Jesus as wholly divine, beyond human, and so, we imagine, compassion and forgiveness would demand no human effort from him; being wholly divine He would be immune from human suffering as well as from human emotions. But have we forgotten the shortest sentence in the Bible, found in John 11:35: 'Jesus wept'? Jesus wept when He heard the news of the death of His beloved friend Lazarus.

At the centre of our Christian faith is the incarnation: God became one of us, fully human. St Paul states this clearly in his letter to the Philippians:

> Let the same mind be in you as was in Christ Jesus,
> who, though he was in the form of God,
> did not regard equality with God
> as something to be exploited,

but emptied himself,
taking the form of a slave,
being born in human likeness.
And being found in human form,
he humbled himself
and became obedient to the point of death –
even death on a cross.[15]

In the accounts of the life of Jesus in the New Testament, we see and hear His feelings expressed as He engages with humanity, both with individuals and with community. Ronald Rolheiser, the spiritual writer, asks, 'What does God's power look like? How does it feel as God in this world?' As we consider the relationship between compassion and forgiveness we need to ask ourselves how it would feel to experience and identify with Jesus' feelings in the world.

If you have ever been overpowered physically and been helpless in that, if you have ever been hit or slapped by someone and been powerless to defend yourself or fight back, then you have felt how God feels in this world. ...

---

[15] Philippians 2:5–8, NRSVA.

If you have ever felt like a minority of one before the group hysteria of a crowd gone mad, if you have ever felt, firsthand, the sick evil of gang rape, then you have felt how God feels in this world ... and how Jesus felt on Good Friday. ...

God never overpowers. God's power in this world is never the power of muscle, a speed, a physical attractiveness, a brilliance, or a grace which (as the contemporary expression has it) blows you away and makes you shout: 'Yes! Yes! There is a God!' Worldly power tries to work that way. God's power though is more muted, more helpless, more shamed, and more marginalised. But it lies at a deeper level, at the ultimate base of things, and will in the end gently have the final say.

To work for justice and peace in this world is not to move from being Mother Teresa to being Rambo or Batman. The God who undergirds justice and peace beats up no one and His or Her cause is not furthered when we do.[16]

[16] Ron Rolheiser, *Holy Longing: The Search for a Christian Spirituality* (NY: Doubleday, 1999) p. 184–185.

Jesus suffered. Jesus was hurt. Jesus was betrayed and denied by His closest followers. Jesus was abused and humiliated. Jesus was falsely accused, and yet, even as He hangs on the cross, we see His compassion. And as His followers we must ask ourselves what His example from the cross calls on us to do.

Jesus was ritually humiliated. A crown of thorns was roughly fashioned and forced onto His head. A purple robe was thrown over His open wounds. He was publicly mocked, laughed at, jeered at. Then He was made to carry His own cross through the streets. Finally, He was cruelly nailed to that cross between two convicted criminals.

And how did Jesus react? He reacted by forgiving those who had inflicted all that pain and humiliation on Him.

'Father, forgive them; for they know not what they do.'[17]

His words are filled with His compassionate understanding of His tormentors' terrible actions.

---

[17] Luke 23:34, KJV.

Forgiveness offered to an individual or a group has been described as life being lived at its fullest. Moments from death, Jesus is living His life at its fullest. He didn't say, 'Father, forgive them; they should have known better.' He said, 'Father, forgive them; they are not responsible for their actions.' He understood why they did what they had done, even though they themselves did not understand their own actions. The incarnated Jesus understood the actions and feelings of sinful humanity. He understood that they were ignorant of the full enormity of their cruelty and their violence.

We experience Jesus' extraordinary compassion when He engages with the two criminals who were crucified on either side of Him. One of them, presumably taking his cue from Jesus' tormentors on the ground, tries to humiliate and undermine Jesus by goading Him to save Himself if, indeed, He is divine. Jesus is silent. The other criminal, transcending his sinful nature, and recognising that he is in the presence of the Messiah, asks Jesus to have compassion on him, to remember him when He enters paradise. Even today, the beautiful, generous, forgiving words of Jesus strike us powerfully anew:

'Today you will be with me in paradise.'[18]

Jesus could so easily have put a clear distance between Himself and the criminal on the simple grounds of the criminal's guilt and His own innocence. He could have said, 'You hardly deserve it because of your sinful past, but I've decided to forgive you.' Or he could have said something like, 'I hope I won't regret offering forgiveness to a convicted criminal, but...' But He doesn't. Instead He reaches out to this criminal as His brother, making no distinction between them. This is so much more than pity. This is compassion. This is understanding. This is empathy.

Harper Lee, in her novel, *To Kill A Mockingbird*, defines empathy with crystal clarity through one of the novel's main characters, Atticus Finch, who tells his daughter, Scout, that full understanding of another human being can only be achieved by

---

[18] Luke 23:43.

climbing into somebody else's skin and moving around in it. And this is the very important step we are called upon to take if we are to move from hate to pity and beyond.

Compassion and pity are easily confused with each other, but they are different in essence. The difference lies in detachment. Pity asks us to consider how awful it must be for the person going through the misfortune. Compassion weeps with the person who is suffering, feels what that person is feeling, because compassion has crawled inside that person's skin and moved around in it. We may be separated from those for whom we feel compassion, our relationship with them may be bruised and scarred, but we recognise that we are fellow human beings and children of God. A move from pity to compassion is an admission of our common humanity. A move from pity to compassion is one of empathy together with the understanding that flows from it. It is a clear step towards the 'other'. We can see this in the incarnation with Jesus leaving heaven to come to earth as a human being in order to heal our division from God.

Jackie Pullinger went from England to Hong Kong more than 40 years ago. She started sharing the love of Jesus Christ with gangsters and with those who were poor in the Kowloon Walled City. She bore witness to people who, as they were freed from drug addiction and criminality, were able to start new lives. For Jackie it was not enough merely to tell them about God's love for them; she needed to demonstrate that love by becoming the hands, the eyes, the feet, and the loving, forgiving heart of Jesus in their world.

In the person of Jesus, God has come to us. We still struggle with sin both in our own lives and in the world. Jesus came to us and identified with us in our sinfulness when He stepped into the river Jordan and insisted on being baptised by His cousin, John. So the incarnation is not only about giving humanity a perfect example to follow; it is also about God being willing to identify with humanity's sinfulness. It is about Jesus dying on the cross, forgiving us unconditionally, and ensuring our salvation. A Church of Ireland (Anglican) post-communion prayer reminds us that God has come to us in the midst of our sin: when we were 'far off'.[19]

The moment we begin to engage with compassion is a moment charged with significance. We have left behind the position of hate. Without downplaying the harm which has been done to us, we are beginning to see things differently as we continue to make the journey to forgiveness. We know that we must confront the full enormity of the harm which has been done to us, but we are also aware of the first stirrings of mercy deep within us.

In his letter to the Romans, chapters 12–14, St Paul addresses what it means to live as

---

[19] 'Father of all,
we give you thanks and praise,
that when we were still far off
you met us in your Son and brought us home.
Dying and living, he declared your love,
gave us grace, and opened the gate of glory.
May we who share Christ's body live his risen life;
we who drink his cup bring life to others;
we whom the Spirit lights give light to the world.
Keep us firm in the hope you have set before us,
so we and all your children shall be free,
and the whole earth live to praise your name;
through Christ our Lord.
Amen.' (Emphasis added.)

Christians in our everyday lives. He tells his listeners that their discipleship is to be lived out as a response to God's mercy. He tells us that we are to be 'living sacrifice[s]'.[20] God has been merciful to us, and we are called to show that same mercy to one another. According to St Paul, this is our 'reasonable act of worship' (MOUNCE).[21] When Micah, in his time, spoke to God's people, the Lord challenged them to 'act justly and to love mercy': 'He has shown you, O mortal, what is good. And what does the Lord require of you? To act justly and to love mercy and to walk humbly with your God.'[22]

The challenge comes when we ask ourselves if others deserve to be treated the same way as us. Compassion places us alongside one another. Compassion calls on all of us to look squarely at the harm that has been done to us, and to look equally squarely at the reasons we

---

[20] Romans 12:1: 'Therefore, I urge you, brothers and sisters, in view of God's mercy, to offer your bodies as a *living* sacrifice, holy and pleasing to God – this is your true and proper worship.' (Emphasis added.)

[21] :F. F. Bruce, *'Romans' New Tyndale Commentaries* (IVP 1993), p. 213.

[22] Micah 6:8.

believe are behind the infliction of that harm, and this from the perspective of what we know to be true, which is that God loves us and is merciful to us. In the New Testament we can turn to John, chapter 3, verse 16, and find: 'For God so loved the world that he gave his one and only Son, that whoever believes in him shall not perish but have eternal life.' The incarnation is an awesome revelation of God's love for us, whereby God became fully human, one of us, not in the broken and sinful image we embody, but in the perfect image of Jesus. The incarnation shows us the face of true, perfected compassion: an identification with the other effected through a compassionate understanding and sharing of the other's feelings.

There is justice and there is mercy. Which do you prefer? Which is better, in your opinion? Most of us would acknowledge that our answer would depend on the timing of the question. If you've just been robbed, then justice is what you would want and seek; nothing would get in the way of your need to have the guilty found and punished. If, on the other hand, you've just been stopped for speeding, it is surely mercy you hope will inform the police officer's actions.

Jesus addressed this very issue when He told the parable of the unmerciful servant in Matthew 18.

Then Peter came to Jesus and asked, 'Lord, how many times shall I forgive my brother or sister who sins against me? Up to seven times?' Jesus answered, 'I tell you, not seven times, but seventy-seven times.

'Therefore, the kingdom of heaven is like a king who wanted to settle accounts with his servants. As he began the settlement, a man who owed him ten thousand bags of gold was brought to him. Since he was not able to pay, the master ordered that he and his wife and his children and all that he had be sold to repay the debt.

'At this the servant fell on his knees before him. "Be patient with me," he begged, "and I will pay back everything." The servant's master took pity on him, and cancelled the debt and let him go.

'But when that servant went out, he found one of his fellow servants who owed him a hundred silver coins. He grabbed him and began to choke him. "Pay back what you owe me!" he demanded.

'His fellow servant fell to his knees and begged him, "Be patient with me, and I will pay it back."

'But he refused. Instead, he went off and had the man thrown into prison until he could pay the debt. When the other servants saw what had happened, they were outraged and went and told their master everything that had happened.

'Then the master called the servant in. "You wicked servant," he said, "I cancelled all that debt of yours because you begged me to. Shouldn't you have had mercy on your fellow servant just as I had on you?" In anger his master handed him over to the jailers to be tortured, until he should pay back all he owed.

'This is how my heavenly Father will treat each of you unless you forgive your brother or sister from your heart.'[23]

Jesus, through this parable, is reminding all of His followers that we are a forgiven people. It is only when we understand the loving, forgiving nature of God that we can begin to live

---

[23] Matthew 18:21–35.

out the loving, forgiving message of Jesus. The unmerciful servant begged for mercy for himself, received it, and then failed to show that same mercy to his fellow servant. He failed to make the connection between his generously forgiven self and his fellow servant's need for the same generous forgiveness. What ought to have been a flow of mercy springing from the forgiven one to the one needing forgiveness was blocked by the wicked servant's failure to empathise with his terrified fellow servant. We all need compassion. Jesus identified with our sin, even though He Himself was without sin, and until His last breath His life was about compassion, forgiveness and healing.

Is it possible for us, do you think, who have experienced the abundance of God's compassionate understanding and forgiveness, to take even a small step towards the forgiveness of those who have sinned against us?

For further reflection

- Is it possible to feel compassion for someone who has harmed us?

- What does Jesus' example on the cross call us to do?

- Do others deserve to be treated the same as us?

Chapter 4
Forgiveness

A good idea until you are the one forgiving.

I wonder if you have turned to this chapter first? If you have, let me encourage you to go back and join us at the start. While your journey may take a little longer, you will travel a more rewarding path. If you have travelled with us from the beginning then you know that we have come some considerable distance to reach this point; and we hope you have a clearer view of the concept of forgiveness. The heart of this book is not to find a better definition of forgiveness, but rather a desire to help you live out the reality of forgiveness. Is forgiveness still a distant destination that you hope to reach, or a gate through which you hope to pass on your way to a further destination?

As the saying goes, 'It takes two to tango.' When we consider forgiveness we see quickly that it cannot be a solitary affair: it takes two, the person who has caused hurt and the one to whom hurt has been caused. These two are always present in any consideration of forgiveness. Even when forgiveness is neither sought nor accepted, these two will always be present.

The Christian apologist C. S. Lewis commented after World War Two how forgiveness is considered a good thing unless you have somebody to forgive.[24] This book is not a 'How to Forgive in Ten Easy Steps' manual; forgiveness doesn't work like that. This book is an attempt to consider what forgiveness means for our relationships. In truth, it is hard for us to live healthy lives when forgiveness is absent. So, how does forgiveness shape our lives? If you are a Christian, how does forgiveness affect how you follow Jesus?

---

[24] C. S. Lewis, *Mere Christianity* (London: Fount, 1952) p. 101.

Forgiveness gives us the freedom to be reconciled without settling scores. It allows the hope of the future to define our journey, rather than the pain of the past. Bob Goff, in his book, *Love Does*, tells the story of a Ugandan judge who was assigned to hear cases which related to children who were in jail and waiting for justice.

The children glanced over their shoulders at their parents, ashamed.

In a brilliant move, the judge asked the children to leave the courtroom before the trials began and wait in another room as he spoke to the parents assembled. The judge knew that there was a much bigger issue that needed to be dealt with in the room before the trials began. The judge spoke to the parents and his admonition was simple: 'Parents, forgive your children.' The judge knew that, guilty or not, the children would not be able to move forward in their lives without the forgiveness of their parents. A short time later, he walked into the room where the children were and said, 'Children, your parents have forgiven you.' The children were brought back into the courtroom and fell into the arms of their parents. They had received what they had needed as much as they needed justice. They had received forgiveness.[25]

When Peter asked Jesus if seven was an appropriate number of times to forgive someone who had sinned against him, he probably expected Jesus' unqualified approval. After all, seven times was good, beyond what would have been asked of him by the other religious teachers of the day. Seven is a perfect number with scriptural significance; Peter, one can imagine, would have allowed himself a degree of self-satisfaction. Jesus' answer, 'I tell you, not seven times, but seventy-seven times',[26] challenged Peter as to why he would keep a record of the number of times he was prepared to forgive another. Jesus' message is clear: true forgiveness is a state of heart. The number of times a person has wronged us is not the important factor here. Compassion and understanding have taken up residence in the

---

[25] Bob Goff, *Love Does* (Nashville, TN: Thomas Nelson Publishing, 2012), p. 180.

[26] Matthew 18:21–22.

forgiving heart and will refuse to allow finite numbers to limit that heart's capacity for generosity.

Some people in our lives can hurt us repeatedly and we may find it really hard to forgive them. Why should we forgive them? We can easily find ourselves experiencing renewed anger at the very thought of them. And what about the people who deny any need for our forgiveness, who neither want it nor look for it? Jesus' challenge to Peter can seem too much for us. God calls us to forgive everyone, every time. We are not told what Peter's face looked like when Jesus told him to stop counting and keep forgiving. What we do know is that Jesus' words have caused many of us to struggle in the face of the challenge they pose. How can we forgive what we believe to be the unforgivable? Why should we forgive what we believe to be the unforgivable? And yet, embracing forgiveness allows our journey to be shaped by the hope of the future rather than by the pain of the past. Forgiveness will not ignore what has happened; it acknowledges it, and yet robs it of any power over us.

In the parable of the unmerciful servant, that earthly story with a heavenly meaning which we have discussed earlier, we discover where we are meant to find the strength to forgive.[27] God is the merciful king of the parable, the generous forgiver. God is not indifferent to our sins; they matter to Him, and yet He forgives us. The character and actions of God must shape our behaviour as His disciples. God loves us even in the full glare of our sin, and offers us His generous forgiveness. Jesus does the same when confronted by the woman caught in the act of adultery. In the full glare of her sin, Jesus, after showing up the hypocrisy of those present, offers her forgiveness and a directive to sin no more. Jesus doesn't want us to be tethered to our pain. His Father, the God of love, puts no limit on His forgiveness; can we, His disciples, limit our forgiveness towards others?

In 1997 Sir Chay Blyth held the first Atlantic Rowing Race, an ocean rowing race from the Canary Islands to the West Indies. During the 2005 season when the majority of the boats had completed nearly a third of the race, there was a

---

[27] Matthew 18:21–35.

prolonged spell of unfavourable rowing conditions. Rather than the typical trade winds which would have been helping the fleet, there were strong westerly winds caused mainly by Hurricane Epsilon. These forced many of the crews to stop rowing completely and to deploy a sea anchor to prevent the boats from drifting backwards. A sea anchor (also known as a boat brake) is a device used to stabilise a boat in heavy weather. Rather than tethering the boat to the seabed, the sea anchor increases the drag through the water and thus acts as a brake. When we refuse to forgive we have a 'sea anchor' attached to our life, which acts as a brake preventing us from moving forwards. We are stuck, unable to move away from the hurt that we cannot or will not forgive. Forgiveness would cut the line and free us into forward motion, but stormy conditions will more than likely still prevail. So the question is, should we or should we not cut the line in a storm? Perhaps we can return with an answer later in our journey!

Bishop Tom Wright has written, 'There are people who need to know what God's forgiveness looks like and it is in our lives and relationships where they could, just possibly, be able to experience it. Jesus wanted Peter to learn that we should never, ever give up making forgiveness and reconciliation our goal.'[28] This is at the heart of the parable of the unmerciful servant. God's capacity for forgiveness is limitless. Can we follow God in this? If we can, then our lives may provide a way for others to experience what God's love is like.

Many of us know how difficult it is to forgive. Many of us have struggled in the past, and continue to struggle in the present, with those who have hurt and rejected us. Only by embracing the love of God, and by accepting that God generously forgives us over and over, are we able to forgive others. This is not so much a matter of arriving straightaway at forgiveness, but of deciding that we can no longer stand in the way of God's forgiveness. Expressing God's forgiveness in little things is the fuel we need to forgive greater hurts.

This is a helpful way to consider forgiveness. We believe that God takes the initiative to

---

[28] N. T. Wright *Matthew for Everyone Part 2* (Louisville, KY: Westminster John Knox Press 2004) p. 39.

forgive, but we can decide if we are either willing to oppose God's desire for us to forgive each other, or else rejoice in the loving, limitless forgiveness He offers us by being open to the prospect of emulating it. We have seen how Kathleen Chada was willing to leave the forgiving of her husband to God, and perhaps that is the foundation on which our forgiveness of others should rest: to see it first of all as a reliance on God to change our own hearts, as well as changing the hearts and lives of those we need to forgive.

Perhaps it might be useful to return once more to the parable of the unmerciful servant. The parable leaves us appalled that one who has stood trembling before the king, abjectly pleading for mercy, and who has been shown that mercy, should then behave with such merciless cruelty to his fellow servant. We expect the one who has had his debt forgiven to have no trouble forgiving the debt owed to him by another; we expect him to have no trouble identifying with the other's misery and terror. We expect him to make the connection between his own recent dilemma and the similar one in which his fellow servant now finds himself.

Jesus underlines this connection when He presents both servants, in their pleas for mercy, using the same words: 'Be patient with me, and I will pay it back.' Jesus wants His followers to open themselves to the wonder of God's forgiveness, to be changed by it and, under the influence of this change, to change the lives of others. As God touches our lives, we are to touch the lives of others.

God's forgiveness for humanity must be taken into account in any consideration of humanity's forgiveness for itself. We have to ask, 'If we are all fellow servants who have been treated mercifully by our master, shouldn't we give to each other what has been so generously given to us?'

Forgiveness received is often experienced as a gift, but forgiveness given can be experienced as a sacrifice. When Jesus uttered the words, 'Father, forgive them; for they know not what they do,' He was hanging in agony on the cross, thus revealing to us that forgiveness is inextricably connected to suffering and sacrifice. We ought never to trivialise the act of forgiveness or undermine the terrible struggle it can evoke. It is important neither to trivialise forgiveness nor, indeed, to idealise it as an act we are expected to perform promptly as Christians. More and more we can see that forgiveness is a journey to be embarked on. Perhaps this journey does not describe a straight line, either; it is probably an upwardly moving spiral. We are anchored around the love of God, regularly revisiting our pain, but steadily, with God's grace, moving upwards. At times we can be good at forgiving; at other times, not.

Forgiveness can be experienced as a cross to bear, because when we forgive another person, we are, in effect, letting them go free. We are not demanding an eye for an eye, a tooth for a tooth. We are not looking for revenge. We are not going to allow the harm which has been done to us by this person to define our relationship in the future. None of this is easy. Our instinct is to make the offender pay, to make the offender suffer. This is natural in the interests of serving justice, but not in the interests of forgiveness. Forgiveness looks, not for justice, but for freedom from the toxic effects of harbouring hatred. To forgive is to liberate not only the offender, but also ourselves. The one who forgives has to make a conscious decision to let go of the need for revenge and maybe even sometimes the need for justice. This can be a heavy cross to bear, a painful sacrifice. The cross and sacrifice of Jesus bore great fruit; the sacrifice of forgiveness can also bear great fruit. When we forgive others and allow them to go free, the fruit our action offers us is our soul's liberation. Yes, to forgive can be a cross, but to endure that cross and to keep moving forward means that we are no longer being held hostage by our hatred. We are no longer paralysed by our failure to shoulder that cross and move forward.

You know, there are more burdensome things than carrying a cross. The paralysis engendered by bitterness and the desire for revenge can be much more painful than carrying the cross of forgiveness. The refusal to forgive is like living with clenched fists. It is impossible to live, to work, with clenched fists. Try it. It takes a lot of energy to keep your fists clenched, and when they are clenched, it is impossible to carry out even the simplest tasks. Try holding a cup between two clenched fists! When we cannot forgive, we are stuck, paralysed, trying to hold life between clenched fists. When we forgive, we have to bear the sacrificial cross that forgiveness entails. It is a tough choice, and one that many of us cannot make alone. But then, we do not have to travel the hard road of forgiveness alone. Just as Jesus needed help to carry His cross, we too need help when our cross becomes too heavy to bear alone. We need a 'Veronica' to show us pity when we struggle under the cross of forgiveness. We need a 'Simon of Cyrene' to shoulder the weight of the cross with us when it becomes too heavy to bear alone.

There are many works of literature which take as their central character a figure who is hostage to a past trauma. We think of a classic such as *The Count of Monte Cristo* by Alexandre Dumas, or the modern tortured hero, Batman, portrayed by Christian Bale in Christopher Nolan's *The Dark Knight Trilogy*. Neither character can escape his past trauma, and this fact shapes their future, often tragically. Their stories would have been different had they been able to free themselves from their pasts.

We all want to be free, don't we?

But why would we shoulder a cross in order to be free? Why would we accept the weight of a cross? Two thousand years ago a man accepted the weight of a cross. He accepted the weight of the cross so that we might be free. Jesus made the cross a key to freedom. We know that forgiveness leads to freedom. We know that through the cross of forgiveness we are freed from the paralysis of bitterness and revenge.

When Jesus talks about this society shaped by forgiveness He calls it the kingdom of God. In the Gospel of Luke, Jesus' disciples come and ask Him to teach them how to pray. The prayer that Jesus taught His disciples has become central to the life of all Christians, and indeed has come to shape much of our worship. The Lord's Prayer teaches us that our lives are to be kingdom-centred: God's will lived out on earth as it is in heaven. When we look at the words of this prayer, what is clear is that forgiveness is central to it.

He said to them, 'When you pray, say,
"Father,
hallowed be your name,
your kingdom come.
Give us each day our daily bread.
Forgive us our sins,

for we also forgive everyone who sins against us.
And lead us not into temptation."'[29]

In families and communities around the globe we see the importance, the necessity of forgiveness. It allows the painful experiences of the past to be acknowledged without denying peace to the future. When St Benedict wrote the Rule to guide his monks as they lived together in community, he determined that the Lord's Prayer should be said morning and evening, in the offices of Lauds and Vespers.[30] His intention is clear. The community should not allow faults or grievances to fester. The community would go to their beds without dwelling on the faults of others, and no one in the community would be the focus of others' bad feeling.

One of the most powerful modern-day examples of a person who was inspired by Jesus to forgive is Immaculée Ilibagiza. Immaculée is from Rwanda. During the genocide of 1994 her family was murdered. For 91 days, she and seven other women were confined to a small

---

[29] Luke 11:2–4.

[30] *Rule of St Benedict in English*, chapter 13, p. 42.

bathroom in a pastor's house. They couldn't make a sound as they were being hunted by people with machetes out to kill them. In the middle of this horrendous time, Immaculée discovered forgiveness.

One night I heard screaming not far from the house and then a baby crying. The killers must have slain the mother and left her infant to die in the road. The child cried all night; by morning the cries were weak and sporadic, and by nightfall, it was silent. I heard dogs snarling nearby and shivered as I thought about how that baby's life had ended. I prayed for God to receive the child's innocent soul, and then asked Him, 'How can I forgive people who would do such a thing to an infant?'

I heard His answer as clearly as if we'd been sitting in the same room chatting: 'You are all my children ... and the baby is with Me now.'

It was such a simple sentence, but it was the answer to the prayers I'd been lost in for days. The killers were like children. Yes, they were barbaric creatures who would have to be punished for their actions, but they were still children. They were cruel, vicious, and dangerous, as kids sometimes can be, but, nevertheless, they were children. Their minds had been infected with the evil that had spread across the country, but their souls weren't evil. Despite their atrocities, they were children of God, and I could forgive a child, although it would not be easy ... especially when the child was trying to kill me.

In God's eyes, the killers were part of His family, deserving of love and forgiveness ... I took a crucial step towards forgiving the killers that day. My anger was draining from me – I'd opened my heart to God and He'd touched it with His infinite love. For the first time I pitied the killers. I asked God to forgive their sins and turn their souls toward His beautiful light.

That night I prayed with a clear conscience and a clean heart. For the first time since I entered the bathroom, I slept in peace.[31]

When we accept that forgiveness is a cross, and willingly embrace its sacrifice, we choose

---

[31] Immaculée Ilibagiza, *Left to Tell* (California: Hay House, 2006) pp. 118–119.

the road to peace. If we accept that to Martin Luther King Jr hate and violence was a descending spiral, forgiveness is an ascending one. There is a price to be paid in making the ascent, but it is a price worth paying. As we make the ascent we follow in the steps of people like Immaculée, steps which follow the path of Jesus.

There is a saying, 'A rising tide lifts all boats.' We believe that if we cut the line anchoring us to our past hurts and go with the tide of God's forgiveness, we will find ourselves lifted by the tide towards a new future.

For further reflection

- Do you agree with C. S. Lewis' sentiment that individuals consider forgiveness is a good thing unless we are the one called upon to forgive?

- How can forgiveness give you the freedom to be reconciled without settling scores?

- Why does forgiveness replace pain with hope as a means of shaping our journey?

- Can we limit our forgiveness of others?

- Do you agree that forgiveness is inextricably connected to suffering and sacrifice?

Chapter 5
Grace

Friend of the last moment.[32]
Father Christian de Chergé

'Mercy,' we are told, 'is not being given what we deserve, and grace is being given what we don't deserve.' When the Bible talks about forgiveness it often partners it with grace. The American theologian, Paul Zahl, in his book, *Grace in Practice – A Theology of Everyday Life*, wrote:

What is grace? Grace is love that seeks you out when you have nothing to give in return. Grace is love coming at you that has nothing to do with you. Grace is being loved when

[32] Martin McGee OSB *Christian Martyrs for a Muslim People* (Mahwah, NJ: Paulist Press, 2008) p. 93.

you are unlovable. It is being loved when you are the opposite of lovable. …

Let's go a little further. Grace is love that has nothing to do with you, the beloved. It has everything to do with the lover. Grace is irrational in that it has nothing to do with weights and measures. It has nothing to do with my intrinsic qualities or so-called 'gifts' (whatever they may be). It reflects a decision on the part of the giver, the one who loves, in relation to the receiver, the one who is loved, that negates any qualifications the receiver may personally hold. … Grace is one-way love. Take an inventory of yourself. Watch other people about whose happiness you care. You will see it over and over: one-way love lifts up. One-way love cures. One-way love transforms. It is the change agent of life.[33]

If we are seeking to understand forgiveness better, we should now ask, 'Who deserves our forgiveness?' Straightaway we start to think about categories of people we might be able to forgive easily: those who have hurt us

[33] Paul Zahl, *Grace in Practice – A Theology of Everyday Life* (Grand Rapids, MI: Eerdmans 2007) pp. 36–37.

unintentionally; those who have expressed sorrow for having hurt us. However, if we ask the question, 'Who deserves our forgiveness?' the truthful answer is, 'No one!' Nobody has the right to be forgiven. We receive a gift when we are forgiven. Forgiveness is always a gift freely given, never a right to be expected. In other words, forgiveness has its roots in grace.

We can appreciate how beneficial forgiveness can be to the one receiving it: the beloved. We can understand how offering forgiveness cuts the tethers to past pain, and brings freedom. And yet, as we have acknowledged on our journey together, it can be hard to forgive.

Let us consider Jesus' parable of the Pharisee and the tax collector in the temple. The tax collector elicits our pity, perhaps even our compassion, when he prays, 'God, be merciful to me, a sinner!'[34] We can see how we, ourselves, might find it easier to forgive him. But what about others? What about the person who refuses to acknowledge that he has done anything wrong? What about the person who throws our forgiveness back in our face? The

---

[34] Luke 18:13, NRSVA.

person who doesn't want our forgiveness? Should we still offer forgiveness to those people? Grace answers in the affirmative. Grace calls us to love because we have been loved first by God. 'Grace is irrational in the sense that it has nothing to do with weights and measures.'[35]

Jesus, the best teacher on forgiveness in human history, shows us how to forgive before forgiveness is even asked for. Think about the story of Zacchaeus.[36] He wanted to see Jesus. Nothing else. He didn't look for forgiveness for his dishonest ways. He simply wanted to be in the presence of Jesus. Jesus, by choosing to eat with Zacchaeus, makes it clear that He has already forgiven him; and graced by Jesus' forgiveness, Zacchaeus is enabled to repent and change his ways.

To those looking on, Jesus' favouring of Zacchaeus, His unsolicited forgiveness of Zacchaeus, doubtless seemed unfair, undeserved. But this is grace, and grace has nothing to do with fairness. Grace is 'one-way love.' Grace is 'love coming at you that has

---

[35] Zahl, *Grace in Practice*, p. 36.

[36] Luke 19:1–10.

nothing to do with you'. Grace is 'irrational in the sense that it has nothing to do with weights and measures'.

Can we forgive before forgiveness has been asked of us? That's a difficult one! How is it going to be received? Will it be welcomed? It might be thrown back in our face! But are we not better able to deal with that eventuality if our hands are open, than we will be if our hands are clenched into fists? Forgiveness shapes all our relationships if forgiveness is the background to our lives; and this can be challenging to society.

How comfortable is society about fostering a culture of forgiveness? In his 2013 novel, *Born Weird*, Andrew Kaufman introduces five siblings with the surname Weird who feel out of step with the world. Following their birth, each Weird child is blessed but over the course of a lifetime this manifests as a curse. The blessings give the Weirds particular capabilities or predispositions. [37] Angie's blessing of always forgiving becomes a curse for her, because she is manipulated by her siblings. Kaufman skilfully shows how something which appears initially

---

[37] Andrew Kaufman, *Born Weird* (London: The Friday Project, 2013).

as a blessing can turn out to be very costly to the 'blessed' individual.

God's grace and strength enable us to endure the cross of forgiveness. The ability to carry the cross of forgiveness comes from our closeness to God. Our lives find meaning when lived in connection with the life of Jesus. What Jesus taught us by His life, and more especially by His death, was that the cross gives way to the resurrection. Life after forgiveness, whether in this world or the next, is worth the weight of the cross. The reality of the pain of crucifixion is redeemed by the victory of the resurrection. This can be difficult to comprehend before you arrive at forgiveness; in fact, it may be impossible to fully comprehend this side of heaven.

A wonderful example of someone who did see the freedom offered by forgiveness is Christian de Charge. He was a French Trappist monk in Algeria who was martyred along with 16 others for their faith. The film *Of Gods and Men* is based on their story.[38] Christian was a man of forgiveness. Evidence of this is to be

---

[38] John Kiser, *The Monks of Tibhirine: Faith, Love, and Terror in Algeria* (NY: St Martin's Griffin, 2003) p. 245.

found in his written 'Last Testament', which he stated was to be opened and read if he died by violence. The text was opened on the feast of Pentecost, 26th May, shortly after the monks were killed. In it he writes:

If it should happen one day – and it could be today – that I become a victim of the terrorism, which now seems ready to encompass all the foreigners living in Algeria, I would like my community, my Church, my family, to remember that my life was given to God and to this country. I ask them to accept that the One Master of all life was not a stranger to this brutal departure.
...

I could not desire such a death. It seems to me to be important to state this. I do not see, in fact, how I could rejoice if this people I love were to be accused of my murder. It would be to pay too dearly for what will, perhaps, be called 'the grace of martyrdom,' to owe it to an Algerian, whoever he may be, especially if he is acting in fidelity to what he believes to be Islam. ...

And you also, the friend of my final moment, who would not be aware of what you were doing. Yes, for you also I wish this 'thank you' – and this adieu – to commend you to the God whose face I see in yours.

And may we find each other, happy 'good thieves' in Paradise, if it pleases God, the Father of us both. Amen.[39]

Christian describes his would-be executioner as 'the friend of my final moment' and his prayer is to commend him to God so they will find each other and be united in heaven. Surely this act of forgiveness was a cross! Christian desires forgiveness for his executioner. He does not desire martyrdom for himself, nor does he desire the challenge it would be for others to forgive his executioner; yet, he addresses this cross because his life is lived in the context of God's love. In that larger context, forgiveness is possible because of God's grace. The pain of the cross is not eternal. The ability and the strength to bear a heavy burden comes from the grace of God. By His grace God is doing what we, in our brokenness, cannot do. And we are stepping out

[39] http://www.ocso.org/index.php?option=com_docman& task=cat_view&gid=100&Itemid=187&lang=en (accessed 8th December 2016).

of God's way so that He may shoulder the burden of forgiveness.

To forgive, we acknowledge, is difficult. To forgive without God's grace is impossible. To choose not to forgive makes it impossible to live freely. If we make this choice, are we, in effect, holding back God's love? If we are, then we are involved in something which is both exhausting, degrading and futile. Instead, we need to seek God's strength to offer forgiveness when it is neither asked for nor deserved. There is an obvious freedom for the person being offered this forgiveness, but God's grace also frees the forgiver. Their pain no longer holds them in thrall; their energy is no longer expended in withholding God's forgiveness; their future is no longer shaped by their past.

On 8th June 1972, the Vietnam War was raging. A nine-year-old girl, Kim Phúc, was horribly injured when a Napalm bomb was dropped on Trang Bang. As she fled from the bombing, the image of her agonised face and her burning body was captured on camera by photographer Nick Ut, and the image subsequently became the iconic one of the Vietnam conflict. In 2008 Kim recorded a programme, *I Believe*, for the Canadian Broadcasting Corporation. In this programme she said:

> In Christmas 1982, I accepted Jesus Christ as my personal savior. It was an amazing turning point in my life. God helped me to learn to forgive – the most difficult of all lessons. It didn't happen in a day and it wasn't easy. But I finally got it.
>
> Forgiveness made me free from hatred. I still have many scars on my body and severe pain most days but my heart is cleansed.
>
> Napalm is very powerful but faith, forgiveness and love are much more powerful. We would not have war at all if everyone could learn how to live with true love, hope and forgiveness.[40]

When we decide to seek God's strength to live as forgiving people we embrace the power of God to shape our lives. We remove any power pain has over us. We will no longer lose energy keeping the memory of the trauma alive. Forgiving when forgiveness is neither sought

---

[40] http://www.npr.org/templates/story/story.php?storyId=91964687 (accessed 8th December 2016).

nor deserved releases us into a future unencumbered by the pain of the past. It causes us to shift our focus away from our pain to God's plan for our lives, and enables us to see the transformation He is effecting in our lives because of His love for us. 'Grace is one-way love ... You will see it over and over: one-way love lifts up. One-way love transforms. It is the change agent of life.'[41]

This book may seem like an attempt to make forgiveness and everything associated with it appear neat and logical: a straightforward journey. We have left a place of hate for a place of pity. From pity we journeyed to compassion, and then onwards to forgiveness. Yet experience often teaches us that a difficult journey is seldom straightforward, and it is for that reason we have visualised forgiveness as an upwardly moving spiral.

The Chapel of Thanksgiving in Thanksgiving Square, Dallas, rises as the focal element on the eastern side of the square. The white 'spiral of life' constructed of white marble aggregate suggests the 'up-reach of the human spirit'. Inside the chapel, the spiral is topped with the

---

[41] Zahl, *Grace in Practice*, pp. 36–37.

stained glass 'Glory Window', one of the largest horizontally mounted stained-glass pieces in the world. You can see this window on the cover of this book. The window features brighter colours as the spiral reaches its apex, becoming brighter as it reaches the centre. It is a beautiful representation of the journey that God is calling us to make in forgiving others.

Matthew records Jesus saying, 'Come to me, all you who are weary and burdened, and I will give you rest. Take my yoke upon you and learn from me, for I am gentle and humble in heart, and you will find rest for your souls. For my yoke is easy and my burden is light.'[42] Grace enables us to lay down the burden of an unforgiving heart, and to acknowledge that Jesus has already granted forgiveness. Grace is the point on our journey when we hear Jesus' invitation: 'Come to me, all you who are weary and burdened, and I will give you rest.' Grace is one-way love.

---

[42] Matthew 11:28–30.

For further reflection

- Paul Zahl would have us see grace as one-way love: from the lover to the beloved. What do you think?

- When we consider someone who doesn't want our forgiveness, should we still forgive?

- Thinking about the story of Jesus and Zacchaeus, can we forgive before we are asked?

- Do you think that the ability to carry the cross of forgiveness comes from God being close to us?

- Does Jesus' invitation to come to Him help you share the burden of forgiveness with Him?

Chapter 6
Peace

Works of love are works of peace.[43]

Does forgiveness mark the end of our journey? Do we stop at forgiveness and pitch our tent there? No, forgiveness is not an end in itself, but the means to an end. Our real destination is peace. In this chapter we're going to view our destination, even though it might still seem far away.

The path to peace is revealed by forgiveness. What is peace? Is it simply the absence of war, the absence of turmoil? If it is, then division can still survive alongside peace. Avoidance of the

---

[43] This is the name of a book published by Ignatius Press recording in photographs the apostolic work and prayer life of the Missionaries of Charity.

'other' alone could ensure such an absence of turmoil. The truth is that peace cannot be arrived at so easily. Peace cannot prevail unless division is eradicated. When there is division there can be no real peace. Peace creates unity, and unity reveals the presence of peace. It is the positive presence of God's will and purposes perfectly expressed: God's Shalom.

Peace does not legislate for parallel living; it does not legislate for the avoidance of friction by the abolition of any encounter between divided humanity. Peace exists in the dynamic interdependence of a healthy society. It is not good enough to live apart from those who are different from us. Peace requires us to live together in mutual regard and respect, thriving on what unites us. Is that too demanding? Forgiving another person may seem only possible if you never have to have contact with that person again. A kind of forgiving and forgetting! Peace demands that we forgive and remember. Forgiveness remembers. We remember that the other person is a child of God and our brother or our sister. How can there be peace if we are estranged from a member of our own family?

You would be forgiven for feeling that the journey to peace is too difficult. It is difficult enough even with God's grace to forgive a person, but now there is the further necessity to fully encounter that person. This may be far too much for some, and understandably so, but peace must remain the aim of our journey: our destination. The hard truth is that if we fail to fully encounter the 'other', true peace will remain elusive.

When Peter asked Jesus how many times he should forgive his brother, Jesus' answer implied that Peter's whole life should be immersed in forgiveness. Jesus wanted Peter to experience peace. He wanted Peter to see that to have peace he must enter into relationship with others. Even when others have caused us harm and our encounter with them begins with trauma, we can heal that trauma by the act of forgiveness. Peter remembered and counted the faults; Jesus wanted him to remember God's love, and forgive.

For Jesus, forgiveness is foundational to peace. Forgiveness opens our lives to new possibilities. When we are unable to forgive, we grow scar tissue which restricts and limits us.

We become stunted, paralysed. Think of the husband whose wife has had an affair. Think of the woman who has been raped. Scar tissue grows over the wound, a permanent reminder of what they have suffered. Future encounters with others are often jeopardised, blanketed in suspicion, distrust, bitterness. Forgiveness removes the scar tissue and restores the possibility of future emotional and physical engagements with others. Restrictions are dissolved by the freedom that forgiveness brings. Fists become unclenched to open and interact again with the world. They are unclenched to create, to feel, to caress. Forgiveness can open the door to peace as it shapes our lives into the hope of a better future.

How can that hope of peace become a reality? How can any encounter with the one who has hurt me be peaceful? How can I encounter my enemy? Am I being foolish or am I being courageous? The truth probably is that I am being both. The story of the Catholic Church in Algeria shows how forgiveness shapes our peace and makes room for hope. The Algerian Christians chose peace when they faced the humiliation of persecution and death. The

Church lost everything. At one time it had been a powerful institution, running schools and hospitals. Over time these powers were taken aggressively from the Church. All the foreigners in the country were asked to leave, and since the Church was for the most part a missionary Church, this request to leave had a direct effect on it. By staying, the missionaries were risking their lives. Those missionaries who stayed in Algeria suffered the humiliation of losing their jobs in the schools and hospitals they had built, and having to look for new jobs in state-run institutions. They lived in fear for their lives all the time. The obvious and most sensible choice seemed to be to leave the country. The missionaries could have become angry or defensive. They could have become ashamed, humiliated at their loss of power and position. They could have abandoned Algeria and bitterly condemned it, while feeling justified in their actions for the rest of their lives. They chose to stay. Humiliated and under threat, they stayed in what was now a very dangerous environment.

The reason they stayed is summed up in the term 'sacrament of encounter'. This 'sacrament of encounter' emerged as a direct fruit of the Church in Algeria choosing to stay in the country despite the humiliations heaped upon them. They chose to remain and to enable others to encounter Jesus by their example. Their theory was a simple living out of Paul's words: 'You [together] are the body of Christ'.[44] They did not want to convert Muslims. They did not want to fight, so they neither became defensive nor did they hide. They simply wanted Jesus, through the quality of their lives, to be present to the people of Algeria. Martin McGee OSB, in his book, *Christian Martyrs for a Muslim People*, explains the demands of the 'sacrament of encounter':

> This new approach or emphasis on encounter, what the Church in Algeria calls the sacrament of encounter, is much more demanding of the missionary, as the quality of his own life becomes the key to the proclamation of the Gospel. In the past, the sacraments worked regardless of the person administrating them. Now the sacrament of encounter depends on the person's

---

[44] 1 Corinthians 12:27.

closeness to God, on him being a clear medium through which the love of God is passed on to another person, and on his receptivity to accepting God's love from another person. This requires much more from the missionaries than simply answering the questions or putting up new buildings, however necessary these answers may be. The effectiveness of this sacrament depends on the transparency of Christ's presence and love in the individual Christian and in his or her community.[45]

Those who are hurt and in pain, and who choose to forgive the instigators of the pain are, in effect, saying that they refuse to define themselves in terms of their pain. Forgiveness allows us to acknowledge the painful encounter, and yet walk away from the restrictions it may seek to impose. The path we take to peace is not one of avoidance but one of encounter. Forgiveness grants new possibilities of finding peace even in the midst of pain. The effectiveness of the sacrament of encounter 'depends on the transparency of Christ's

---

[45] McGee OSB, *Christian Martyrs for a Muslim People*, p. 67.

presence and love in the individual Christian and in his or her community'.[46]

St Benedict knew peace was important in a healthy community. He sought to guide his monks who were living in community to live at peace with one another. What St Benedict addressed in his monasteries also needs to be addressed in our society as a whole. It is a challenge for us to be at peace, to live together as brothers and sisters. But failure to do so breeds inequality, war, violence, bitterness and competition. As we encounter one another, we are called to be people of peace. Instead of feeling helpless in the midst of a world at war, we need to ask ourselves every night, 'How much peace did I contribute to the world today? Did I speak words of peace? Did I live out actions of peace? Was my thinking today formed from attitudes of peace?'

For Jesus calls us to be people of peace.

It is easy to love peace when we live in a peaceful society. Jesus called His disciples not just to love peace, but to make peace. In other words, as disciples of Jesus we are called upon

---

[46] McGee OSB, *Christian Martyrs for a Muslim People*, p. 67.

to confront division and to make peace. Consider the world's growing need for electricity which is environmentally friendly. Consider the drive to install solar panels, not only for our own needs, but also so that we can contribute to the national grid. Jesus taught us that being peacemakers calls us to address the divisions around us, not only to make our individual lives more peaceful, but also to contribute to the international peace grid.

To be a peacemaker is to acknowledge the tenderness which resides at the heart of humanity, however much humanity tries to harden itself against that tenderness. We are made in the image of God and Scripture reveals to us that compassion is the essence of God's nature, and the heart of God is defined by its tenderness.

Patrick Mathias, a psychologist who was based in L'Arche Trosly, France, for more than 25 years and who died in 2007, describes tenderness like this:

> Tenderness is a bringing together of being. It carries security as it soothes fears of abandonment, loss or isolation. It affirms each person. It strengthens the other in their

sense of existence and upholds their value. It is the emotional current of exchanges giving meaning to meetings which neither persecute nor devour.[47]

When we are tender and establish peace, we break down the walls which divide. The mentality of 'us' and 'them' is eroded. Brother Henri Verges, a Trappist monk who was martyred in Algeria, said, 'Rather than just tolerating others, we must try to find God's gift to each individual so that we can marvel at it.'[48] This is the challenge at the heart of building peace! When this is our guiding principle, when we try to discover the unique God-given gift in the other, we become a united, peaceful community. Our identity is the truth about who we are, and that identity should never be a prison of our own choosing, a self-incarceration to which we stubbornly commit. Our identity must be a life-giving fountain of tenderness.

---

[47] Jean Vanier showed this passage to Paul in correspondence at a conference in Trosly.

[48] McGee OSB, *Christian Martyrs for a Muslim People*, p. 34.

This is the gift of living in true peace, and the fruit of this gift is hope.

For further reflection

- How would you describe peace in terms of what it makes manifest as opposed to simply being the absence of conflict?

- In what way does peace demand we forgive and remember?

- What would the 'sacrament of encounter' look like in your own life?

Chapter 7
Hope

Never be afraid to trust an unknown future to a
known God.
Corrie Ten Boom

Hope is future-orientated. It urges us towards
something we don't yet possess. For Christian
believers, this hope comes from God's promised
peace and it urges us towards that peace. 'Who
hopes for what they already have?' was St Paul's
question to the young church in Rome.[49]

On New Year's Eve, millions of people will
sit down to write their New Year's resolutions.
You may well be one of them. In that simple
action, they are painting a picture of the future
as they want it to be. That picture will be their

---

[49] Romans 8:24.

inspiration for the coming year. Their hope springs from a vision telling them that this year will be different. Forgiveness frees us from being imprisoned by the past, and the future-facing vision of a better life gives us fresh hope. Travelling with hope urges us towards a promised future. If you have made it to this chapter, then we trust that you have already seen the possibility of peace and have heard the faint harmonies of hope.

Christian hope has a certainty because of the One who makes the promise. Corrie ten Boom said, 'Never be afraid to trust an unknown future to a known God.'[50] We cannot know what tomorrow will bring, and yet we can accept the unknown, because of what we do know about our Father God. Father Jacques Philippe has said:

> He who accepts to put everything into the hands of God, to allow him to give and take according to his good pleasure, this individual finds an inexpressible peace and interior freedom. ... This is the way to

---

[50] Corrie ten Boom, *Clippings from My Notebook* (Nashville, TN: Thomas Nelson, 1982).

happiness, because if we leave God free to act in his way, he is infinitely more capable of rendering us happy than we ourselves are, because he knows us and loves us more than we can ever know or love ourselves.[51]

Hope is a God-focused and God-empowered attitude for our journey.

God calls each of us to be shaped by the hope that our past need not limit us. We are not anchored to past trauma and pain. Instead we can experience a freedom to look to the future with hope. Christian discipleship is rooted in the belief that we shall fully experience God's peace. The hope is that this peace will offer us the strength we need as we struggle to live as Jesus' disciples in a fallen world. Our journey in hope is the opposite of Martin Luther King Jr's violent 'downward spiral'. Our direction of travel is

---

[51] Father Jacques Philippe, *Searching for and Maintaining Peace* (NY: Society of St Paul, 2002) p. 38.
Jacques Philippe was born on 12th March 1947 in Lorraine, France. After studying mathematics in college, he spent several years teaching and doing scientific research. In 1976, he met the then recently founded Community of the Beatitudes and answered the Lord's call to follow Him through this vocation.

upwards, an 'upward spiral' like the one so beautifully represented in the stained glass 'Glory Window' of the Chapel of Thanksgiving in Dallas, Texas. Hope is the axis around which our spiral climbs. Hope provides the space to believe that we can remember our past without our future being shaped by its pain alone.

Forgiveness cuts away our bonds. In the complex history of Great Britain and Ireland, the visit of Queen Elizabeth II to the Republic of Ireland in 2011 was a significant moment. In a speech given in Dublin Castle she said:

> Madam President, speaking here in Dublin Castle it is impossible to ignore the weight of history, as it was yesterday when you and I laid wreaths at the Garden of Remembrance. Indeed, so much of this visit reminds us of the complexity of our history, its many layers and traditions, but also the importance of forbearance and conciliation. Of being able to bow to the past, but not be bound by it.[52]

---

[52] www.govtiq.com/Queen85Editorials/IrishDinnerSpeech.pdf (accessed 15th December 2016).

We have already seen how forgiveness must begin by naming that which needs to be forgiven. It is named in the hope that once exposed, it can be healed: a bowing without the binding. At times our journey has led us to where we were reluctant to go. We have had to look into the shadows and confront the hidden.

Robert remembers, as a student, asking for directions to the cathedral in Kilkenny only to be told with complete sincerity, 'Oh, if I was going there I wouldn't start from here!' No one chooses a traumatic experience, but acknowledging our need for forgiveness, and our need to give forgiveness, begins at the point of our pain. Hope for a better future cannot be based on the pretence that we have never been hurt. The hope that God will create a new peace begins when forgiveness addresses our brokenness. Although we will continue to carry scars, they need not restrict us. We need not be limited by hurt. Our destination gives us hope; our pain is not the whole story; it is not even the whole chapter.

This book seeks to nurture hope even when it is fragile. Hate, pity and compassion, forgiveness and grace are steps on the way.

Peace is our longed-for destination, and hope is our constant companion.

In the Gospel of Mark we meet a man whose hope brings him to Jesus. He's called Jairus. He is a father who believes that Jesus can heal his daughter. Imagine the intensity of the hope which takes him from his daughter's bedside. She lies near to death but, hope-fuelled, he leaves her to search for Jesus! 'Then one of the synagogue leaders, named Jairus, came, and when he saw Jesus, he fell at his feet. He pleaded earnestly with him, "My little daughter is dying. Please come and put your hands on her so that she will be healed and live."'[53]

Jairus' hope comes from his faith. The only thing that would take a father from the bedside of his little girl, as she lies dying, is hope. Such is its power! He hopes to see his little girl well and whole. He leaves the source of his pain to go to the source of his hope. Jairus was desperate for the presence of Jesus. As disciples we make a similar journey. The journey can be difficult but our first step is to bring Jesus into the place of pain, just as Jairus did.

---

[53] Mark 5:21–43.

When we suffer in life we carry with us the frailty of our wounds. Those wounds can be reopened by a word, an experience. They can bleed afresh from a traumatic encounter. We hear of a person 'nursing a wound'. It conjures up a picture of an individual cradling a broken arm to protect it from further harm. When what we fear is further emotional wounding, we can protect ourselves by hardening our hearts, turning our hearts of flesh and blood into hearts of stone. However, hope reaches past our defences and lays gentle hands on our wounds. Forgiveness heals bleeding wounds of the past. Mark tells us that when Jairus came to plead for help, 'Jesus went with him.' How different would Jairus' return journey be to his outward one! We can imagine his hope mounting with every step. He has found Jesus and Jesus has agreed to accompany him home.

Jairus' journey can be our journey. There is new hope travelling with Jesus, travelling with the hope that things will get better, that wounds will be healed.

And I heard a loud voice from the throne saying, 'Look! God's dwelling-place is now among the people, and he will dwell with them. They will be his people, and God himself will be with them and be their God. "He will wipe every tear from their eyes. There will be no more death" or mourning or crying or pain, for the old order of things has passed away.'[54]

[54] Revelation 21:3–4.

For further reflection

• How are hope and trust connected in our journey of forgiveness?

• Why is it important to remember that forgiveness begins with a naming of what needs to be forgiven?

• Where did Jairus' hope come from, and how can his journey become ours?

Postscript: Afterword

My yoke is easy and my burden is light.[55]

At this stage you have come to the end of our book, but not to the end of your own journey. I hope that your encounter with the themes will help you as you travel onwards.

Encounter and relationship are at the heart of this little book, born out of the friendship between the authors and from our encounters with the society that has shaped us. In a single day of life we will have many encounters and hopefully most of these will be positive and affirming. The reality of life will mean, however, that some of those encounters will be bruising experiences and indeed may even leave a scar. Jesus understood life; it holds no surprises for

---

[55] Matthew 11:30.

Him. So, to prepare His disciples for their encounter with the world, He taught them to forgive. Foundational to our journey as authors has been our shared Christian faith; and the assertion that God is travelling with us, our source of strength. As modern-day disciples of Jesus Christ, we need His reply to St Peter when he came to Jesus and asked, '"Lord, how many times shall I forgive my brother or sister who sins against me? Up to seven times?" Jesus answered, "I tell you, not seven times, but seventy-seven times."'[56]

Whether a society is divided or united depends on its individual members. In this book we have invited you to join in our honest encounter creatively. Our world often calls us to forget the past so we can move forwards unencumbered by it. Alongside our assertion of the need of creative, honest encounter is our plea not to forget. 'Forgive and forget' is not the way forwards. Rather we believe that the maxim should be 'forgive and remember'.

Whether it is at the level of society, family or individual, forgetting is often impossible. So a

---

[56] Matthew 18:21–22.

truth that echoes throughout our journey is a call to remember. We are not calling you to strive to achieve peace by developing amnesia: no! Our journey has called us to look more closely at the source of our pain and to apply the salve of forgiveness. It may 'smart', but it has a healing quality. The pain is not forgotten, but transformed as part of a wider healing process.

We offer this book to be a companion as you travel onwards. Remember that at times you may need to forgive yourself. We haven't said much about this in the book but it remains an important aspect of healthy living.

We leave you with the Lord Jesus' invitation as a means of reminding you that at the heart of our struggle with forgiveness is the cross, where both pain and redemption are present:

'Come to me, all you who are weary and burdened, and I will give you rest. Take my yoke upon you and learn from me, for I am gentle and humble in heart, and you will find rest for your souls. For my yoke is easy and my burden is light.'[57]

---

[57] Matthew 11:28–30.